CELEBRATING THE CITY OF JERUSALEM

Celebrating the City of Jerusalem

Walter the Educator

Silent King Books

SILENT KING BOOKS

SKB

Copyright © 2024 by Walter the Educator

All rights reserved. No part of this book may be reproduced in any manner whatsoever without written permission except in the case of brief quotations embodied in critical articles and reviews.

First Printing, 2024

Disclaimer
This book is a literary work; the story is not about specific persons, locations, situations, and/or circumstances unless mentioned in a historical context. Any resemblance to real persons, locations, situations, and/or circumstances is coincidental. This book is for entertainment and informational purposes only. The author and publisher offer this information without warranties expressed or implied. No matter the grounds, neither the author nor the publisher will be accountable for any losses, injuries, or other damages caused by the reader's use of this book. The use of this book acknowledges an understanding and acceptance of this disclaimer.

Celebrating the City of Jerusalem is a little collectible souvenir book that belongs to the Celebrating Cities Book Series by Walter the Educator. Collect them all and more books at WaltertheEducator.com

USE THE EXTRA SPACE TO TAKE NOTES AND DOCUMENT YOUR MEMORIES

JERUSALEM

In Jerusalem, where ancient stones whisper tales untold,

Celebrating the City of Jerusalem

Beneath a sky that cradles dreams both young and old,

A city woven from the threads of history and divine,

Where faiths converge, their sacred paths entwine.

Upon the Temple Mount, where prayers rise like smoke,

Echoes of the past in every word that's spoke,

The Western Wall stands solemn, steadfast, ever true,

A silent witness to the centuries it has lived through.

In the labyrinthine alleys of the Old City's heart,

Cultures blend and diverge, yet never truly part.

Celebrating the City of
Jerusalem

Muslim, Jew, and Christian tread these cobbled streets,

Each step a testament to where history repeats.

The Dome of the Rock, resplendent in the sun's bright beam,

Gleams like a beacon in a prophet's dream.

Its golden dome, a crown upon the city's brow,

A symbol of the sacred then, and the sacred now.

Mount Zion whispers secrets in the olive groves,

Where David's harp still strums in ancient troves.

The psalms rise up, ethereal, as shadows wane,

Celebrating the City of Jerusalem

In every leaf, a note of a heavenly refrain.

Gethsemane, where olive trees gnarled and old,

Bear witness to a night of sorrow, brave and bold.

In every branch, the echoes of a sacred plight,

Of prayers whispered softly in the stillness of the night.

Jerusalem's markets, bustling, full of life,

Vendors call, spices swirl, scents cut like a knife.

Silk and pottery, relics of a vibrant trade,

In every stall, a tapestry of history is laid.

From the heights of the Citadel, one sees it all,

The rise and fall of empires, the city's timeless call.

Crusaders, kings, and caliphs have all laid claim,

Yet Jerusalem remains, steadfast and the same.

The Kidron Valley, where shadows stretch and yawn,

Holds the dreams of countless, from dusk until dawn.

Tombs and stones mark the passage of the years,

Each one a testament to hopes, joys, and fears.

In Mea Shearim, traditions tightly cling,

Stories of the past through each echo ring.

Hassidim in black coats, tall hats, and prayer,

A living history in the open air.

Celebrate Jerusalem's enduring grace,

In her sacred stones, every sacred place.

A city of dreams, where history and future blend,

A timeless story, with no end.

Celebrating the City of Jerusalem

ABOUT THE CREATOR

Walter the Educator is one of the pseudonyms for Walter Anderson. Formally educated in Chemistry, Business, and Education, he is an educator, an author, a diverse entrepreneur, and he is the son of a disabled war veteran. "Walter the Educator" shares his time between educating and creating. He holds interests and owns several creative projects that entertain, enlighten, enhance, and educate, hoping to inspire and motivate you. Follow, find new works, and stay up to date with
Walter the Educator™ at
WaltertheEducator.com.

www.ingramcontent.com/pod-product-compliance
Lightning Source LLC
LaVergne TN
LVHW012048070526
838201LV00082B/3858